Hummingbirds

by **Steven Otfinoski**

mc **Marshall Cavendish**
Benchmark
New York

Thanks to Bill Hilton, Jr., executive director of the Hilton Pond Center for Piedmont Natural History,
for his expert reading of this manuscript.

Marshall Cavendish Benchmark
99 White Plains Road
Tarrytown, New York 10591-5502
www.marshallcavendish.us

Text copyright © 2009 by Marshall Cavendish Corporation

All Web sites were available and accurate when sent to press.

Library of Congress Cataloging-in-Publication Data

Otfinoski, Steven.
Hummingbirds / by Steven Otfinoski.
p. cm. — (Animals animals)
Summary: "Provides comprehensive information on the anatomy, special
skills, habitats, and diet of hummingbirds"—Provided by publisher.
Includes bibliographical references and index.
ISBN 978-0-7614-2932-6 (alk. paper)
1. Hummingbirds—Juvenile literature. I. Title. II. Series.

QL696.A558O84 2008
598.7'64—dc22
2007024325

Photo research by Joan Meisel

Cover photo: Tim Davis/Corbis

The photographs in this book are used by permission and through the courtesy of:
Alamy: Danita Delimont, 6; Kevin Schafer, 7; Roger Eritja, 11; Marco Secchi, 38; Alistair Scott, 40.
Animals Animals - Earth Scenes: Richard Day, 9; Alan G. Nelson, 22; Jacq Wilburn, 25. Corbis: Joe McDonald, 1;
George D. Lepp, 16, 18, 21; Ron Austing, Frank Lane Picture Agency, 26; Eric & David Hosking, 34;
Annie Griffiths Belt, 36. *Photo Researchers, Inc.:* Gerald C. Kelley, 4; Kenneth W. Fink, 10; Anthony Mercieca, 27.
VIREO: J. Turner MD, 12; Doug Wechsler, 14; K. Schafer, 19.

Editor: Joy Bean
Publisher: Michelle Bisson
Art Director: Anahid Hamparian
Series Designer: Adam Mietlowski

Printed in Malaysia
1 3 5 6 4 2

Contents

1 Jewels in Flight

Big gifts sometimes come in little packages. That is certainly the case in the world of birds. The hummingbird is the smallest bird in the world and is one of the most unique. A list of the hummingbird's achievements reads like a record book. For starters, there are about 340 *species*, or kinds, of hummingbirds, making them the second-largest bird family. Hummingbirds are found only in the Western Hemisphere, which includes North, Central, and South America. Only about seventeen hummingbird species live and breed in the United States.

Hummingbirds are among the most colorful of birds. Their bright, dazzling colors shine like jewels in

Hummingbirds are very small; some species are smaller than the flowers they eat from.

The bright green and blue colors on this broad-billed hummingbird make it stand out from the flowers it feeds on.

Did You Know . . .
The South American nation of Ecuador has 163 species of hummingbirds, more than any other country.

the sunlight. Early Spanish explorers of the Western Hemisphere called them *joyas voladores,* Spanish for "flying jewels," when they first saw them. Hummingbirds' iridescent feathers match the vibrant hues of the flowers they drink *nectar* from. They are also the only birds that can fly vertically and backward and can hover for long periods in midair. How do they do it? Hummingbirds' wing muscles are extremely powerful and make up 30 percent

6

*A hummingbird's wing muscles are very strong and allow it to hover
in the air.*

Species Chart

◆ The ruby-throated hummingbird is the only hummingbird that lives east of the Mississippi River and north of Florida. It is less than 4 inches (10 centimeters) long and weighs only 0.11 to 0.14 ounces (3 to 4 grams). That is about two-tenths the weight of a first-class letter. It has green feathers on its upper body. Only the adult male has a red throat. Females have white throats, as do young males.

Two ruby-throated hummingbirds feed on flowers.

◆ The giant hummingbird is, not surprisingly, the largest hummingbird. It is 8.25 inches (21 cm) in length and weighs 0.7 ounces (20 g). It makes its home in the Andes Mountains of South America.

While smaller than most other birds, the giant hummingbird is the largest of all the species of hummingbirds.

The bee hummingbird is the smallest of all the species of hummingbirds, weighing less than an ounce.

◆ At the other end of the spectrum is the bee hummingbird, the smallest bird in the world. It is just 2.25 inches (5.7 cm) long. Half its length is made up of its bill and tail. It weighs about 0.09 ounces (2.8 g) and is found only on the island of Cuba.

The ruby-throated hummingbird migrates a long distance every year and flies the distance nonstop.

of their body weight. They also have a unique rotary joint at the shoulder that allows them to change direction easily with their long, narrow wings.

Hummingbirds are one of the fastest birds for their size. They have a normal flying speed of 25 to 30 miles (40 to 48 kilometers) per hour, but can dive at up to 65 miles (105 km) per hour. Hummingbirds are also the long-distance champions when it comes to *migration.* The ruby-throated hummingbird annually flies nonstop from the coastal United States, across the Gulf of Mexico, and then into Mexico and Central America, where it spends the winter months. Just the trip across the gulf is a total distance of about 500 miles (805 km). The ruby-throated hummingbird flies this distance nonstop in eighteen to twenty hours. But that is a short trip compared to the long 3,000-mile (4,828-km) migration of the rufous hummingbird, which flies from its breeding grounds from the Pacific Northwest to Alaska to its wintering ground in sunny Mexico. Some rufous hummingbirds cover a distance of 12,000 miles (19,312 km) during a round-trip migration. It is one of the longest migration routes of any bird.

The fast beating of a hummingbird's wings makes a humming sound.

14

How can these tiny birds make such a long journey? Besides their powerful wings, they bulk up before the long journey. The ruby-throated hummingbird, for instance, nearly doubles its body weight, storing away enough body fat to fuel it on its long flight without it having to stop and eat.

Because of their amazing feats and gorgeous colors, humans have been fascinated with hummingbirds for a long time. People watch in awe as the tiny birds dart from flower to flower, making a low humming sound with their rapidly beating wings that gave them their name.

Hummingbirds are truly one of nature's most awesome creations.

2 Always Eating

Where does the hummingbird get all the energy it needs as it flits through the air? It gets its energy from two main food sources—the flower nectar and tiny insects. Just as the hummingbird relies on the flower's sweet nectar to give it strength, the flower depends on the hummingbird to carry on its body the flower's dustlike *pollen* to other flowers, *fertilizing* them and helping to create new flowers.

The hummingbird has little or no sense of smell, so it can only find the flowers through its keen eyesight. Many flowers that depend on hummingbirds for pollination have developed bright colors, particularly red, that attract hummingbirds and stand out against the green of nature.

Hummingbirds eat the nectar of flowers as well as insects for energy.

An up-close view of a hummingbird's beak shows us how long and thin it is.

Many of the flowers with the sweetest nectar have blossoms so deep that most birds cannot reach the pool of nectar inside with their bills. But that is no problem for the hummingbird. Its bill is long and slender. It can reach deep into flowers. Its tongue is long, too. It is also split into two parts at the tip. When the bird sticks its tongue into the pool of nectar, it forms a little spoon at the tip that it uses to hold the nectar. When the hummingbird sticks its tongue back into its mouth, the nectar flows down into its throat. The bird can take thirteen licks with its tongue in a second. The hummingbird also eats tiny insects on the flowers and catches others midair.

Eating is usually a full-time job for the hummingbird. Its fast *metabolism* requires frequent refueling in the form of food. Except when migrating, the

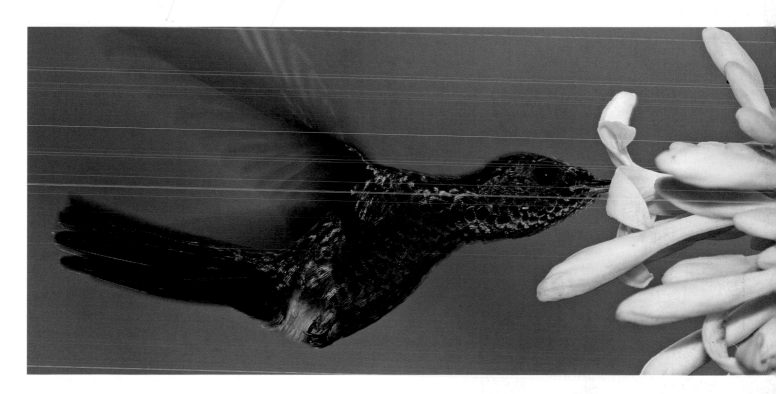

In order to keep its belly full, a hummingbird must eat constantly during the day.

hummingbird is never more than a few hours from starvation and must eat every ten minutes—or more frequently—during the day. Each tiny meal may last only thirty seconds to a minute, but it is a necessity. If deprived of food for just ninety minutes, a hummingbird can lose up to 15 percent of its body weight.

During cool nights, the hummingbird may slow down its system so it can rest and not have to eat. It goes into a trancelike state called *torpor*. It becomes very still. Its heartbeat drops from its normal rate of 1,260 beats per minute to only about 50 beats. If you were to see a hummingbird in torpor, you might think it was dead. But it is just resting. When morning arrives, the hummingbird will become active and start visiting flowers again for nectar. It will also go into torpor when it is under great stress. Torpor is one of the hummingbird's most important survival tools.

In winter almost all hummingbirds in the northern regions head for warmer places. They migrate by flying south, sometimes for hundreds of miles. In the spring, the same birds will return to their northern homes. Often the flowers are not yet in bloom when

Did You Know . . .
Hummingbirds, unlike other birds, are unable to walk on the ground. They use their tiny feet to perch on the branches of trees.

20

When hummingbirds cannot find flowers to eat from, they will feed on tree sap.

they arrive. When that is the case, they stick their long bills in holes in trees made by other birds and fill up on the sugary tree *sap* until the flowers blossom.

3 Little Hummers

The mating season for hummingbirds is earlier than it is for most birds. In the western United States it can start as early as December and run through February. The ruby-throated hummingbird returns to the United States and Canada in late March and begins to mate then. Courtship starts with the males putting on dazzling displays of their flying skills to impress a female. The fearless males swoop, dip, and dive through the air at speeds up to 65 miles (104.6 km) per hour. The sunlight reflects off their brightly-colored throats as they dive through the air. The

When looking for a mate, male hummingbirds use their flying skills to impress females.

sound of their feathers against the wind creates a bird hum. The male that most impresses the female will be chosen as her mate.

Mating takes place in a shady, leaf-covered spot. Once it is over, the male and female go their separate ways. The male may find another female to mate with. The female will spend up to a week building her tiny, cup-shaped nest. She often makes it on a tree branch and may build the new nest on the previous year's nest. She uses soft grass, shreds of leaves, and cattail fluff as material and uses spider webbing to bind it all together. The female lines the inside of the nest with bird feathers and cotton seeds to make it soft. She attaches bits of moss and lichen to the outside to *camouflage* the nest so that it will look like part of the tree to passing *predators*, mostly other birds.

When the nest is finished, it is time for her to lay eggs. She usually lays just two tiny white eggs in the nest. Hummingbird eggs are the smallest of all bird eggs and are no bigger than a jellybean. The mother spends most of her time sitting on the eggs to keep them warm. She leaves the nest only to feed on the nectar of the nearest flowers. In two to three weeks

A hummingbird's nest is made of soft material like grass and cattail fluff.

the babies break out of their eggshells. These tiny *nestlings* are black in color and have no feathers. Their eyes are tightly shut. The mother begins to feed them at once. She collects insects and nectar in a part of her throat called the *crop.* There the food is softened so that the nestlings can easily eat it. Returning to the nest, the mother sticks her long bill deep into each little hummer's throat and injects a portion of the softened food from her crop. She will repeat this process many times each day.

After about sixteen days, the little hummers will have grown feathers, and their eyes will have opened.

Hummingbird eggs are so small, a nest of them can fit in the palm of an adult's hand.

*A mother hummingbird will feed her babies until they have the strength
to fly to flowers on their own.*

This hummingbird chick practices flapping its wings. Soon it will be able to fly away from the nest on its own.

They are now called *fledglings* and are ready to practice flying from the edge of the tiny nest to the nearest flowers to drink nectar on their own. They stay with their mother in the crowded nest a while longer. By early fall, the young hummingbirds are ready to fly south and live on their own. They will be ready to find a mate of their own by the next spring.

Most hummingbirds live only three to five years in the wild. Those in captivity live considerably longer, up to twelve or even fifteen years. Hummingbirds may be kept in zoos, where they can be properly cared for, but it is illegal for an individual to keep a hummingbird in captivity in the United States. It is even against the law to possess a hummingbird nest or hummingbird feathers or another part of the body.

If you ever find an injured hummingbird or a baby that fell out of its nest, you should immediately call your local wildlife rehabilitation center, another wildlife agency, or a veterinarian for help.

4 Small But Feisty

Hummingbirds may be small, but they are feisty. If they or their nestlings are threatened, they will attack birds of prey much larger than themselves, including blue jays, hawks, and crows. Blue jays are about three times the size of an average hummingbird and hawks can be five times as big. The hummingbird will dive through the air and whiz by the intruder. Its angry buzz and swift flight may lead the predator to mistake it for a hornet or a wasp. Perhaps afraid it will be stung, the bigger bird may fly away.

In most cases, birds of prey will rarely go after a hummingbird. Hummingbirds are too fast to be caught easily and are too small a meal for the birds to

The blue jay is one of the hummingbird's greatest predators.

bother with. Preying birds will, however, eat humming-bird eggs and young hummers, as will snakes and small animals. Luckily, the female hummingbird usually camouflages her nest so well that predators do not find it.

Weather and climate are a far greater threat to the hummingbird's survival than are other predators. Because they have a poorly insulated and fragile body, hummingbirds are often at the mercy of sudden shifts in weather. Extreme cold or a long rainfall can hurt or kill them. A drought that withers flowers will leave them without nectar and in danger of starvation.

More permanent climate changes are causing some hummingbirds to adapt their migratory patterns. As the winters become warmer in many regions of the United States, hummingbirds are showing up in places where they were never seen before. The calliope hummingbird, the smallest hummingbird in North America, is commonly found in the western states. In 2000, a calliope hummingbird was seen for the first time in New Jersey. The following year two calliopes were sighted in New York State. Then in December 2006 a female calliope was spotted by excited bird-watchers in

Did You Know . . .
Hummingbirds are so small that they have been known to occasionally fall prey to large insects, such as praying mantises. Sometimes they even get trapped in the webs of large spiders.

Cold weather or lack of rain can make flowers wilt, which threatens a hummingbird's survival.

Climate changes can cause hummingbirds, like this calliope, to find a home in areas they are not normally found.

Connecticut. Other species have been sighted in the eastern United States. Since 1985, at least eighteen Rufous hummingbirds have been sighted in Ohio. A total of twelve different species have been reported in North and South Carolina since March 2003. Warmer winters and the loss of *habitat* in Mexico, where many calliopes and other hummingbirds spend the winter, may be responsible.

5 Hummingbirds and People

People are fascinated by hummingbirds. Many people put out red-colored feeders filled with homemade "nectar" made of sugar water in their backyards or plant red-colored flowers in their gardens to attract the tiny birds.

People are rarely a direct threat to hummingbirds, but the environment they attract the birds to can be dangerous. The windows of houses and garages are a serious threat. The hummingbird, like other birds, sees the reflection of the outdoors in the window and not the window itself. It will fly straight into the glass and be stunned or even killed.

Red feeders attract hummingbirds to people's yards.

A window reflecting the outdoors can con-fuse a hummingbird.

Another danger is garages. The hummingbird will be attracted to the red handle of the door release, mistaking it for a flower. It flies into the open garage and does not know how to get out again. Its instinct is to fly upward, not outward, and it quickly becomes trapped. Within an hour, the exhausted hummingbird dies. A person who finds a hummingbird in this frantic state should attempt to catch it gently in his or her cupped hands. It will lie still until released in the open air.

Another long-term threat to hummingbirds are the poisonous chemical sprays and herbicides used to kill pesky insects and weeds in farm fields. By killing off the insects, the sprays deprive hummingbirds of a main source of food. If the sprays get into flowers and plants, hummingbirds can *ingest* them when drinking the flower's nectar.

Global warming was mentioned earlier as changing the migratory patterns of calliope hummingbirds. Soon other hummingbirds may be flying east, drawn by the warmer winters. While many bird lovers will be excited to see these birds for the first time, this geographic shift poses a danger to the hummers. They may find few if any flowers yet in bloom, despite the warmer temperatures. Backyard feeders alone will

Spraying pesticides on plants can hurt hummingbirds, which may eat from a sprayed flower.

not be enough to sustain them, and many of these new migrants will die.

One other danger to ruby-throated hummingbirds is the loss of habitat in their breeding range in the United States and Canada. When natural areas are replaced by new buildings, hummingbirds have nowhere to go.

Ruby-throated hummingbirds and other species feed on particular flowers. When these flowers are destroyed by human development they cannot adapt to eating different flowers and have no food source. Some of the species of hummingbirds that are on the critically endangered list today are the chestnut-bellied hummingbird, the sapphire-bellied humming-bird, and the Honduran emerald hummingbird.

Despite these potential problems, the general outlook for most hummingbirds is good. It is likely that these fascinating "flying jewels" will be around for a long time to delight us.

Glossary

camouflage—A technique used by animals to conceal themselves by blending in with their surroundings.

crop—A pouch in the throat of birds in which food is held in order to be brought back up and fed to babies.

fertilize—To make a plant able to reproduce by uniting male and female cells.

fledgling—Young bird that has just learned to fly.

habitat—The place where an animal lives, including the living and nonliving things in the environment.

ingest—To take food or liquid into the body.

metabolism—The processes by which an animal burns up the energy obtained from food.

migration—The act of passing regularly from one region to another, usually in response to seasonal weather changes.

nectar—The sweet juice of a flower or plant.

nestling—Bird too young to leave the nest.

pollen—Fine grains produced by flowering plants that can fertilize other plants.

predator—Animals that prey on, or eat, other animals to survive.

sap—A watery juice that circulates in a plant or tree.

species—A group of animals that share the same characteristics and mate only with their own kind.

torpor—A trancelike state of inactivity entered by some animals to conserve energy.

Find Out More

Books

Berger, Bruce. *A Dazzle of Hummingbirds*. Montrose, CA: London Town Press, 2005.

Fogden, Michael. *Hummingbirds of Costa Rica*. Richmond Hill, Ontario, Canada: Firefly Books, 2006.

Howell, Steve. *Hummingbirds of North America: The Photographic Guide*. Princeton, NJ: Princeton University Press, 2003.

Kelly, Irene. *It's a Hummingbird's Life*. New York: Holiday House, 2003.

Sargent, David M. and Sue Rogers. *Hummer Hummingbird*. Ozark, MO: Ozark Publications, 2003.

Sovak, Jan. *Learning About Hummingbirds* (Dover Little Activity Books). Mineola, NY: Dover Publications, 2004.

Web Sites

Hummingbirds.net
http://www.hummingbirds.net

Hummingbird Facts
http://www.wbu.com/edu/hummer.htm

The Hummingbird Web Site
http://www.hummingbirdwebsite.com

Hummingbird World
http://www.hummingbirdworld.com

Operation Ruby Throat: The Hummingbird Project http://www.rubythroat.org

Index

Page numbers for illustrations are in **boldface**.

About the Author

Steven Otfinoski is the author of many books on animals. He has written five books in World Book's award-winning Animals of the World series. He has also written *Koalas*, *Sea Horses*, *Alligators*, and *Skunks* in the AnimalsAnimals series. He lives in Connecticut with his wife, a high school teacher and editor.